This book is primarily a work of fiction. The names, characters, places and incidents are based on the author's imagination. Financial concepts are based on fact and the author's opinion.

First paperback edition 2018

ISBN 978-0-9977910-5-1 (paperback)

Eleven Digital Group, LLC
New York, NY
info@elevendigitalgroup.com

Visit us at bullbearkidsbooks.com

Adventures in Finance with Bull & Bear

Investing for the Future

Created By: Roy & Susan Kim
Illustrated By: Surendhra K. Padayatchi

In memoriam:

To Susan's father, John G. Westcott
January 5, 1943 – September 5, 2017
Husband, "Grumpa", Patriot
Thank you for your love, support, intelligence and sarcasm.
We will think of you every trip to the beach.

Bull and Bear were on a ship vacationing somewhere fun. They worried about NOTHING except all-you-can eat candy, playing and sun.

The ship was a playground - it was crazy, fun, and grand. Endless activities, delicious treats, and even a beach with sand!

"I could do this every day," said Bull as he floated in the pool.

Bear agreed, "No work or school. Just playing would be cool!"

Suddenly an annoying voice interrupted their fantasy. "You know your trip will end soon - it is only temporary."

He continued, "A life like this is expensive. Nothing is ever free. Last I checked, and you should know, money doesn't grow on trees."

Bull and Bear were super annoyed, but "Mister Know-It-All" was right. Their savings wasn't enough and paradise was out of sight.

A grandpa was listening nearby. He chuckled and offered advice. "Start investing when you're young and when you retire you can live nice."

Bear talked into her cell phone, "search for investing on the net." Some information was easy to learn and others hard to get. The phone said, "investing is when you buy something now and hope it grows in the future.

When you sell it for more than you paid, your savings will grow even bigger."

Bear said, "How do we decide where to invest with so many choices out there?!"

Bull didn't have an answer. He just looked at Bear with a blank stare.

A parent relaxing by the pool was listening to Bull and Bear. She said, "excuse me for interrupting, but I have advice I can share."
She continued, "I am a wealth manager – I help people invest their money.
If you need help investing, you hire professionals like me."

"What you invest in depends on a lot of facts. For instance, how much money you can invest, how much you're willing to lose, and when you need your money back."

"For younger people like yourselves who are starting to invest, I recommend mutual funds and E-T-Fs."

"Buying one of these is like investing in a lot of companies. This is called diversifying - the most important thing you will learn from me.
Never put all your eggs in one basket. If something goes wrong, you'll lose lots of money, and wish you never did it."
CRUISE
CRUISE

A tired worker chimed in and offered his own advice.

"Pay attention kids, and invest wisely, or you'll work your ENTIRE life."

Bull and Bear left the pool. They were worried but mostly better.

They were back to thinking about their future - sunny beaches and warm weather.

Their trip eventually ended, and being back at home was sad. Their first day back at work was terrible, tiring, and BAD! Bull said, "It's time we start investing! Working forever makes me cry. I'll work hard today and invest wisely so there's more time to enjoy life."

Bear agreed, and started her research. She learned a lot on their trip. She did what she does best and searched the Internet for more tips.

They found a program online that helped them invest. They answered questions about themselves, and the computer did the rest.

Bull and Bear smiled. Now they have a plan for when they retire. Eventually they could stop working and do whatever their hearts desire.

Bull exclaimed, "When I retire, I'll live on a ship and eat tons of treats each day!"

Bear laughed, "I'm going to travel the world and have new adventures in every city."

Investing wisely is as important as learning your ABC's. Important topics you should learn - diversification, risk, and the time value of money.

Remember that diversifying is a smart thing to do. Investing in a mutual fund or E-T-F will help do this for you.

When you invest, there's no guarantee that you'll get your money back. There's a chance you can lose money. Understanding risk will protect you from that.

Remember that risks come with rewards and you won't always win. Risks mean that something bad can happen, but that's why you're diversifying.

The money you invest today should grow over the years.

The value may go up and down, but be patient and try not to fear.

Invest it, don't touch it, add to it, and watch it grow.
If you don't have time to watch your investments, consider hiring a pro.
We've only touched the surface about how you should invest. Go research and ask questions. You have time to learn the rest.

Don't miss the other adventures in our series...

Visit us at BullBearKidsBooks.com

Glossary

We know that some of the terms in this book are more complicated than others we have written, but they are important to investing. This glossary explains some of these terms and hopefully will help answer any questions you have.

Investing – Committing money to a business, project, or other asset ("investments" or "things") with the expectation of getting more money in return later on in time either in income, or gain from the sale, or both.

Risk – The level of uncertainty that you lose some or all of your money when investing. There are no guarantees when it comes to investing.

Diversification – Investing in multiple things at the same time so you DO NOT have all your risk in one thing. In other words, you don't have all your eggs in one basket.

Time Value of Money – A dollar in your hand today is worth more than a dollar you will receive in the future, because you can invest that dollar today and earn more money (interest) over time. Prices tend to go up as you get older, and you need more dollars to afford the same things in the future.

Mutual Funds & Exchange Traded Funds (ETF) – These are popular and easy ways to make one single investment in many things at once. Imagine a jar filled with different types of candy. In this example, the jar is the mutual fund or ETF, and each piece of candy is a different business, project, or investment.

Money Activities

Hey kids! Here are some activities to help you learn more about money and investing. On the next few pages you'll find matching games, word searches, puzzles and more for you to enjoy.

When you finish these activities, ask your parents to help you visit the Bull & Bear Academy at BullBearKidsBooks.com for more **FREE** activities.

MONEY MATCH

Instructions:
First, look at the words and the coins. Draw a line to match a word to the correct coin. Next, look at the coins and the values. Draw a line to match a coin and the correct value.

<u>**Words**</u>	<u>**Coins**</u>	<u>**Values**</u>
Penny		**$0.05** **5¢**
Quarter		**$0.25** **25¢**
Dime		**$0.01** **1¢**
Nickel		**$0.10** **10¢**

WORD SEARCH

Instructions:
Search for the words in the list below. Circle a word when you find it. Have fun!

List:

Investments	ETF	Diversification
Stocks	Risk	Interest
Bonds	Return	Retirement
Mutual Funds	Reward	Gain

Q	W	E	R	T	Y	U	I	O	P	I	U	Y	T
A	B	B	O	N	D	S	G	H	R	Y	N	M	Z
A	S	Z	V	B	N	M	G	F	D	T	Y	U	V
Z	D	G	T	T	S	E	R	E	T	N	I	L	D
S	D	R	M	E	Z	X	C	V	B	N	N	Y	I
R	R	D	F	T	Q	W	T	Y	I	O	V	M	V
Z	A	E	T	F	B	G	E	J	L	Y	E	Q	E
Z	W	R	T	Y	A	S	D	F	G	H	S	J	R
V	E	L	T	D	N	W	U	O	Z	Z	T	N	S
T	R	E	T	U	R	N	W	R	N	S	M	F	I
N	T	J	D	W	H	S	A	T	Y	U	E	J	F
E	A	G	R	N	C	D	E	U	O	D	N	Z	I
M	G	W	Y	M	P	F	J	K	F	D	T	A	C
E	M	U	T	U	A	L	F	U	N	D	S	N	A
R	H	J	S	E	H	D	J	K	L	T	R	M	T
I	R	A	D	G	J	Y	R	W	O	V	N	M	I
T	Z	I	X	C	V	F	R	C	N	J	H	D	O
E	T	Y	S	U	I	O	K	Q	Z	N	V	H	N
R	R	G	J	K	Z	S	C	D	E	J	I	U	X
A	E	T	J	L	P	U	V	X	Z	D	E	A	F
A	E	Y	I	G	F	M	T	U	O	Z	S	H	G

WORD SEARCH

Instructions:
Search for the words in the list below. Circle a word when you find it. Have fun!

List:

Gain	Money	Index
Loss	Dividend	Exchange
Value	Finance	Wall Street
Portfolio	Market	Ticker

A	W	A	L	L	S	T	R	E	E	T	P	A	P
S	K	Q	K	A	Y	U	F	L	F	U	I	S	C
D	D	D	A	H	T	Q	F	T	S	E	T	D	C
F	I	W	P	J	W	W	F	S	C	T	E	F	S
G	V	F	Q	D	S	E	G	N	Q	E	F	G	H
H	I	Y	P	X	G	R	A	W	G	W	X	S	X
J	D	E	O	C	A	N	Y	P	J	Q	S	Q	Z
K	E	N	I	E	I	Y	T	F	L	O	A	E	V
L	N	O	Y	F	N	U	R	S	L	S	H	T	W
P	D	M	A	F	T	I	E	X	O	D	R	I	F
O	S	H	S	H	L	E	G	N	A	H	C	X	E
I	A	C	D	Y	K	O	W	G	G	F	M	K	J
U	N	V	W	Y	H	P	Q	K	C	G	N	G	R
Y	U	E	R	V	P	O	R	T	F	O	L	I	O
I	Y	D	U	Z	T	R	H	Q	F	H	V	Z	W
T	N	H	G	L	E	C	G	R	G	J	A	C	G
E	R	D	N	Q	A	V	F	B	E	K	S	H	B
W	E	A	E	M	S	V	D	Z	J	K	I	I	K
Q	F	E	C	X	A	B	S	V	E	L	C	P	V
C	B	T	X	N	T	E	K	R	A	M	P	I	Q
B	M	K	Z	V	S	M	A	M	N	M	U	M	T

SECRET MESSAGE

Instructions:
Use the decoder below to read the secret message.

Legend:

A	B	C	D	E	F	G	H	I	J	K	L	M
1	2	3	4	5	6	7	8	9	10	11	12	13

N	O	P	Q	R	S	T	U	V	W	X	Y	Z
14	15	16	17	18	19	20	21	22	23	24	25	26

Secret Message:

8	5	12	12	15

11	9	4	19

.

25	15	21

3	18	1	3	11	5	4

20	8	5

19	5	3	18	5	20

3	15	4	5

.

4	15	14

'

20

6	15	18	7	5	20

20	15

19	1	22	5

1	14	4

9	14	22	5	19	20

.

SECRET MESSAGE

Instructions:
Use the decoder below to read the secret message.

Legend:

A	B	C	D	E	F	G	H	I	J	K	L	M
1	2	3	4	5	6	7	8	9	10	11	12	13

N	O	P	Q	R	S	T	U	V	W	X	Y	Z
14	15	16	17	18	19	20	21	22	23	24	25	26

Secret Message:

9	14	22	5	19	20

23	9	19	5	12	25

1	14	4

19	20	1	18	20

23	8	5	14

25	15	21

1	18	5

25	15	21	14	7

.

			'	
4	15	14		20

6	15	18	7	5	20

20	15

4	9	22	5	18	19	9	6	25

!

HOW MANY WORDS?

Instructions:
Look at the word provided below and see how many different words you can come up with. Write your words in the box provided.

Word:

INVESTMENTS

Other Words:

HOW MANY WORDS?

Instructions:
Look at the word provided below and see how many different words you can come up with. Write your words in the box provided.

Word:

DIVERSIFY

Other Words:

WORD PROBLEMS

Instructions:
Solve the following word problems.

Word Problems:

1. You invest $10 that grows to $20 in time. How much did your investments grow/ gain?

2. You get $100 on your 7th birthday and decide to invest it. Your investment grows to $200 sometime in the future. How much did your investments grow/ gain?

3. Alexis has $100 in savings from babysitting. She invests all her money in one thing. Is Alexis diversified? Yes or No.

4. Addison asked her parents to help her find a money manager to invest her $500 savings when she was 10 years old. Addison's investments grew by $500 over time. How much are her investments worth today?

5. Abigail has $100 that she wants to invest. She remembers that diversifying is important and doesn't want to invest $100 in one place. Divide her money across the following investments and make sure to diversify.

Cash	**EFT 1**	**ETF 2**	**ETF 3**
________	________	________	________

Made in the USA
Las Vegas, NV
07 November 2026

57650033R00024